Poems That Say Yes to Life!

First Collection of Poems

Hal Weiss

Vibe Publications
Copyright 2015 Hal Weiss

Published by
Vibe Publications
Copyright 2015 Hal Weiss

No part of this book may be used, reproduced, transmitted, downloaded, or otherwise copied for public or private use without written permission from the author.

All photographs by Hal Weiss
Cover Design by: Maduranga Nuwan at Mnsartstudio on fiverr.com
Edited by Eva Xanthopoulos at authoreva on fiverr.com

Library of Congress Cataloging-in-Publication Data is Available
Published in the United States
First printing 2015

Dedication

To my parents, Alan and Marlene, who gave me unconditional love and laughter, and to my wife, Rita, who is the love of my life and my inspiration for the poem "Missing You."

Introduction

I wrote these poems for myself, and now want to share them through this book. Many of the poems are philosophical in nature. We're all philosophers really.

This book, as well as my first book "Secrets of Warmth," would never have been written if I hadn't participated in "The Forum" from Landmark Education. They would have remained no more than "nice ideas."

The three-day "Forum" course can change lives and it certainly changed mine. My ideas about what is possible changed, and "possibility" itself became more than just a word in a dictionary or a concept. I am eternally grateful for the benefits I received from doing the Forum and the seminars after that. I thank the Forum Leaders, Seminar Leaders, the participants I've met, and I dedicate the poem "Enthusiasm" to Werner Erhard, the man who started it all before the Forum.

Author's Note

To you dear reader, I recommend reading these poems slowly, and perhaps only a few poems per day.

Obviously you may read as many as you wish, in as little time as you wish, but I believe there is value in slowing down the process. Just as you would savor a glass of wine or sip a cup of coffee, you may want to savor some of these poems.

I truly hope you enjoy these poems.

Namaste,
Hal

Contents

Dedication iv

Introduction v

Author's Note vi

Enthusiasm 1

Love 2

Renewal 3

STAR 4

Happiness 5

The Gift 6

Missing You 7

Seeing and Meaning 8

Sedona 9

IS 10

Thanksgiving 11

Now Hear This! 12

Spring Ahead 13

Owed 14

Zen Park 15

Mom's Laugh	16
Infinity	17
Short Defense	18
The Leaf	19
Action	20
Risk	21
Time	22
Aware	23
Q	24
The Tree	25
The Judge	27
Lepitaph	28
Sky	29
Outlook	30
Night	32
Kaaterskill	33
About the Author	34

Enthusiasm

Enthusiasm Is the Spark of Life
that can turn Possibility into Reality.

It is the Triumph of the Excitement of Possibility
over the Fear of Failure.

It does not Exist in Time.

Enthusiasm can only be Generated
by the Self in the Moment, at each Moment.

The Opposite of Enthusiasm is
Resignation and Complaining.

When Enthusiasm is Created,
Fear of the Unknown is Replaced by
the Excitement of what's Possible.

Enthusiasm is Voting "Yes" to Life!

Love

Love is a Great Inner Force
seeking outward expression.

The constantly-being-created energy of Love
needs to be released,
or it turns sour inside the creator.

One needs someone, someones, or something
to take one's Love out on, so to speak.

When you feel lonely, it isn't due to Love
not coming into your life,
It's due to the lack of expression of Love
coming out from you.

Not putting your Love out into the world
transforms it into unwanted internal pressure.

"Loneliness" means you don't see anybody around to let your Love
out on.

Better widen your vision and let it out on everyone!

Renewal

It's Spring!

Rounding a turn, heading for home,
sunlight reflects off a leaf in a tree.

The sparkle catches my eye
and a smile starts inside.

The smile quickly comes to my face;
Life is renewing itself all around.

The trees are opening their umbrellas,
catching so many of the sun's rays.

They show their green in so many hues,
It tickles the eye to see.

It's good to see—

It's good to be!

STAR

It's alright to stand out and be a star.

Don't be afraid to step out and shine.

But don't shine so that you can appear brighter than others.

Shine so you can light the way for others!

Happiness

If you look around for reasons to be unhappy,
you'll never be caught short!

If you look around for reasons to be happy,
you may have to look harder sometimes,
but they're always available too!

If you realize you don't need reasons to be happy,
you can create happiness whenever you want,
and carry it with you wherever you go!

You can carry as much happiness as you want!

It doesn't weigh anything,
so it won't hold you down.

It doesn't take up any space,
so you always have room for it.

Happiness can overflow,
but if it spills onto anyone else,
they won't mind at all!

CARRY HAPPINESS, it's very light!

The Gift

A time there was when you weren't,
A time there will be when you won't.

The time between is a gift you've been given,
The greatest gift the universe can bestow!

Can you look beyond circumstance and usual fear?
Can you see that it's a miracle just being here?

Can you appreciate just being alive on any Given day?
What would life be like if you accepted it that way?

Missing You

Sometimes when you go away,
I think I'll just hang out and play,
yet soon it seems so long a day.

The hours do a very slow burn,
and then I find I really yearn
for nothing more than your return.

And when once more,
your smiling face enters the door,
I smile too as you walk across the floor.

Being together again is a definite treat,
and my heart skips to a happier beat
as I kiss you hello and know I am complete.

Seeing and Meaning

Few have the proclivity
to see things with much objectivity.
Our eyes send rays of expectations,
they don't just passively receive.
On reality they perform vast alterations,
and it's ourselves they do deceive.

We paste meaning on everything, automatically.
Our brain is programmed to do so
quite mechanically.
It appears to us that we're smart as a fox
as we categorize everything in our brain's little box.

We generate our view of the world
through a deceptive sensory mess.
Our feedback loop keeps
objective truth as anybody's guess!

Being full of what we think we know
makes it very difficult to grow.
Our minds stay stuck with what we think is true,
so it's nearly impossible for anything
new to get through.

We compare and judge people—usually quite low.
And we compare the meaning of things
against what we think we already know.
It's a very big challenge to see this—

And a world of difference to let it go!

Sedona

Incredible beauty surrounds.

Stillness allows us to see.

Relax… be still… just be.

Joy Abounds!

IS

There is no is,
there never was,
nor will there ever be.

It's just a thought,
that we all bought,
but that's not easy to see.

Time can't stand still—
it never will—
See the rings in the tree?

We're all in motion,
in this heavenly ocean,

By and by,
I'm you, and you're me!

Thanksgiving

Thinking that you don't have enough
can make the world seem bleak.
Reality isn't causing the trouble,
it's negative thinking that makes you weak.

Counting your blessings
can give you the knack
of eliminating self-pity
from what you think you lack.

When you can see that
nothing in life is owed you,
you can truly appreciate living.
It's then you'll come to realize
Every day is Thanksgiving!

Now Hear This!

The mind wanders... almost without rest.

Strong currents in a sea of circumstance
push the mind in all directions, aimlessly.

When will the captain take control of the ship?

Without direction, the mind will flounder.
Without a map, the ship is lost.

The captain is the only one who can look
past the shoals to chart a course.

The captain is the only one who can take the wheel.

You can take responsibility when you
remember you're the captain.

It's time!

Spring Ahead

Summertime sun's too strong,
yet, the chill of winter lasts so long.
It's springtime that we await,
I think it's peeking at the gate.

Soon little buds will peek through.
A glorious green canopy will open for view.

I look forward to long walks in the park,
more in the light and less in the dark.

I like when the sun kisses the earth;
I like hearing children playing with mirth.

I enjoy baby animals coming in view.
All around us life seems new.

Springtime returns us from winter's slow motion.
It's nature's elixir, a magic potion.

Winter's snow melts away—
we get a longer day,
and we get back to speed in life's great play.

Sights and sounds of spring bring
enjoyment with a flair.
Smell the fresh foliage in the air.
See the birds darting there — and there!

I believe these are some of the major reasons
I consider springtime one of my four favorite seasons.

Owed

Do you see life coming to you, as a given?
Or can you view life as a gift?
In the first way is your own disappointment driven
In the other lies a freedom that gives life a lift!

When you think something's due you
and it's something you don't receive,
having counted on it
would have you grieve.

But even if it does come
and at whatever speed
your enjoyment will be very short-lived
for you've already discounted the deed.

When we check the books where
speed records have been planted,
nothing beats how fast
we take what we have for granted.

Our tricky minds don't focus on what is
but rather on what is not.
So most of us don't take the time
to appreciate what we've got.

Ah— but the ones who do—
They are a truly joyous lot!

Zen Park

Bright blue sky with brush-stroked clouds
layered in a beautiful display.

A father tries to make a kite fly,
running with his child; joining him at play.

The hawk glides upward without effort,
riding thermal air currents in a spiral array.

Butterflies and dragonflies are dancing
on the fields in a seemingly random way.

Children playing in the sandbox
are laughing and enjoying their stay.

I sit here breathing in this peaceful day,
I am filled— and there's nothing to say.

Mom's Laugh

I'm told, and already know, that my laugh is too loud.
This doesn't bother me, it makes me proud.
It was my Mom who gave the laugh to me,
And I can't think of a happier legacy.

From the earliest days I can retrace,
I remember my family at the picture show.
Mom would find something so funny
her laugh would fill the place—
She'd really let go.

My sister and I would slink beneath our chairs
as everyone would turn around,
and we didn't want to face their stares.

Some bruises we tried to duck too,
as mom's hands and elbows went flying
when her sense of humor shone through.

My dad usually caught the brunt of it,
but he didn't really mind;
he seemed to enjoy mom's laughing fit.

Her laugh came out hard like a shrill shout.
And though some gave us odd looks,
I think it helped others let their laughter out.

I'm grateful I caught this laugh from my mom;
it's an area where she really had the knack.
And though I'm sad for those who won't let go,
I'm not going to hold my laughter back.

Infinity

Staring at infinity
is pleasing to the eye.

You can see it looking at a tree
or looking at clouds in the sky.

Enjoying God's infinite variety
pleases the mind and sets it free.

You can enjoy the variety in people too—
I think that's what He wants us to do.

Short Defense

My poems are short—it's not to abort,
I've just said all I have to say.

My pen laid down, there is no frown,
I smile and walk away.

While others embellish, and do it with relish,
I minimize, to say the least.

When more words occur, thoughts start to blur,
Quiet diet turns frenzied feast.

I complete my thought, though not for naught,
and run away from the beast.

Still more words pile on.
Soon my audience is gone.
I thought I was giving them a treat.

They thought my poem thick.
It was making them sick.
To them, it didn't sound very sweet.

I would check all this chaff,
before I make a gaffe,
I should begin to whittle.

Too much word, syllable, and phrase
puts the mind in a daze.
Long poems often say very little.

The Leaf

A leaf unfurls its green
and soon gets kissed by the sun.
With quiet magic unseen,
it shares its oxygen with everyone.

If only the warmth would stay
but the season goes by fast.
Cold tree releases the leaf,
its time in the sun didn't last.

The leaf weaves its way
to the ground
on an invisible pendulum
with nary a sound.

It loses its moisture
after joining its brothers
and forms a thick carpet
with many others.

Animals of the forest
go by in a hustle.
They step on the leaves
and the leaves then rustle.

Only after falling quietly
to the ground,
Only after dying
It makes its sound.

Action

Between the posts called birth and death
stories mount and the action blurs.
Between these posts you draw your breath
and in action is where your life occurs.

Those who stay in action
are the ones who gain satisfaction.
They won't take it easy or choose to snooze—
it's the juice of life they refuse to lose.

Life isn't about griping or complaining.
It often requires sweating and straining.
Life doesn't occur in the stands,
being loud and clapping your hands.

Life's not about boasting or braying,
It's getting on the field and playing.
It's not whether you win or lose,
It's going for the goals you choose.

Though it's not easy, or calm, or tame—
and often there is strife.
The gold is found in engaging the game
and the game is called "life."

Risk

Take risks or die!

When there's nothing at stake—there's nothing!
And there's no possibility!
When something's possible, you're at risk.
It's scary, but it's lively.

Comfort and safety may not be all
they're cracked up to be.
Ultimately, maybe comfort and safety
are as much fun as being in a coma!

Create goals and go for them,
— you risk not getting them.

If you don't go for them,
you're certain not to get them.

Being at risk is being alive!

Communicate with people what's true for you,
— you risk not being understood!

If you don't communicate, no one can ever
come close to understanding you.

You can't be really alive without really communicating!

The only real risk to being alive is withholding communication—
and not creating and going for your goals.

Take risks or die!

Time

Do you know that time is short?
Have you given it much thought?

Don't miss the beauty of a cloud;
It can't be seen beneath a shroud.

Why seek the comfort of your bed
When a blanket of stars floats overhead?

God paints the sky both day and night
Your eyes to enjoy a glorious sight.

Beauty exists beyond words.
Joy exists beyond thought.

Now go enjoy the songs of birds
For time cannot be bought.

Aware

At any moment of my life,
I'd rather be aware of being alive
than receive the greatest gifts
the richest kingdoms could provide!

You may find that in the end,
when the reaper comes to call—
just that you were given life,
was the greatest gift of all!

Q

Where are we going?
Where are we from?

The questions beckon
the answers won't come.

We search for meaning
where there is none.

What unfillable emptiness
this gnawing unknown!

Best to enjoy life
and leave what's outside alone!

The Tree

The last time I tried to hug a tree,
I was traveling about 30 mph on my skis.
Another skier crossed my path, and rather
than impacting him and drawing his wrath,
I looked for a different course to steer
and toward the forest I started to veer.

But, alas, the forest is made of trees
and a rather large one had its eyes on me.
There was very little time to choose.
At this speed if I hugged that tree,
all recognizable features I'd lose.

I didn't really want to hug the tree;
as it went between my skis it frightened me.
The fastest thought ever went through my mind,
told me to jump and now was the time.

As things were about to go really bad,
I jumped up and to the right
with every bit of strength I had.
The next sensation I came to know,
was my face being smashed into hard-pack snow.

My friends came up fast,
their voices filled with dread.
When they saw the human helicopter,
they were sure I'd be dead.

With broken goggles and a bent pole
I got up very slowly,
surprised to find myself still whole.

Windmilling through the air was really a thrill,
but the next time I hug a tree,
I'll enjoy it much more just standing still.

The Judge

I thought I knew about right and wrong
in myself and other people too.

Yet, eventually everyone was guilty
by the judge that was in me.

Then I remembered the quote,
"Forgive them, they know not what they do."

And letting go of my judgments
it was I who was set free!

I wouldn't waste my energy trying to judge a tree.
Why waste it then judging the people I see?

When I accept people for who they are
I feel more energy and am happier by far.

Judgment is supposed to come from above.
When I give up judging, what I experience is Love!

Lepitaph

Lived Long
Loved Life.

Looked at Lilacs
Listened to the Loon.

Learned a Little
Laughed a Lot.

Learned to Live
and Let Live.

No Longer Longing
Lately, Laying Low.

Sky

Ever-changing patterns in the sky
seem to fill a need in the I.

Clouds remind us everything changes;
nothing's really set.

It's good to remind us—
we seem to forget.

When the sky gets dark,
some get moody of mind.

Patient ones know that beauty returns
and the sun again will shine.

The beauty in the sky is incredible,
ineffable, satisfying, and thrilling.

When you know to look there—
when you're willing.

Lucky ones know the best things are free.
The sun, moon and stars among them—
obviously.

And though it's easy to frown
with your head turned down.

To get a real prize—
Lift your gaze up to the skies.

Outlook

At any moment in time
there may be no reason or rhyme.
Life isn't necessarily the way you see it.
You can only see it
by the way you look at it.

You can look to the light
or you can look at the darkness.
Your feeling will be bright
or there'll be quite a starkness.

And though one seems weak
and the other one strong,
neither way of looking
is right or wrong.

Whether the glass is half full
or there is lack,
what you project out
gets reflected back.

Whether or not you want to,
you color your world with your view.
Whether you're getting joy or strife,
it's your outlook that's determining
the experience of your life.

And your outlook you can shift—
in a split second, if you get the drift.

You're a human with a voice,
rosy-colored glasses, or dark ones...

Your view can come from choice!

Night

Just a quiet little interlude
not really meant to intrude.

Just a little break
for all of us to take.

Just a line of demarcation
like a miniature vacation.

Nighttime seems a mystical, timeless haze
that separates us from our days.

But nighttime is also a magical jewel
where minds and bodies gain strength and renewal.

When life grabs us in its jaws
be grateful for this little pause.

When life chooses us to test
take advantage of our time of rest.

So let our eyelids lumber
and welcome the relaxing slumber.

Tell the mind to cease its chatter
we know full well it doesn't matter.

This "between" time we will borrow
to make us ready for the morrow.

Kaaterskill

I sit upon a scary ledge
where artist's eyes have taken pleasure,
perched dangerously with rocks below
and height at quite a measure.

I sit here shrouded in foggy mist
the scene below obscure,
but I know the beauty that exists
for I've been here before.

A wonderous scene of extraordinary expanse
now hidden from my sight,
perchance the sun will burn the mist
bring beauty back to my delight.

A scene so vast and green
can't be captured by camera or described by pen.
It once filled my eye and enriched my soul
and I long to return here again and again.

Though the view now empty and dull
doesn't bring me down or ruin my stay.
My mind stays meditative and mellow
from the fog's calming way.

And I trust myself to make my way down
from this misty path I shall not stray.
I so want to return here again
I deeply desire another day.

About the Author

Hal Weiss holds a B.S. in Civil Engineering from the City University of New York. He has spent his professional career in the field of civil engineering, most recently managing infrastructure projects throughout the metropolitan New York area.

Hal began his writing career in 1988 with the publication of his first book, "Secrets of Warmth." He started writing poetry in 1986, and continues to write poetry when the muse appears.

When he is not writing or engineering, Hal enjoys listening to a wide range of music, from Baroque to Rock, as well as reading, hiking, skiing, photography and table tennis. Among the people he admires are Nikola Tesla, Buckminster Fuller, Tim Ferris, Dave Asprey, Dr. Jack Kruse, Ben Greenfield, Carlos Castanada, George Washington, Werner Erhard, Dr. Albert Schweitzer, J.S. Bach, and Vivaldi.

Hal is originally from Brooklyn, New York. For the past 20 years, he has lived with his wife in Westchester County, New York.

www.ingramcontent.com/pod-product-compliance
Lightning Source LLC
Chambersburg PA
CBHW061306040426
42444CB00010B/2543